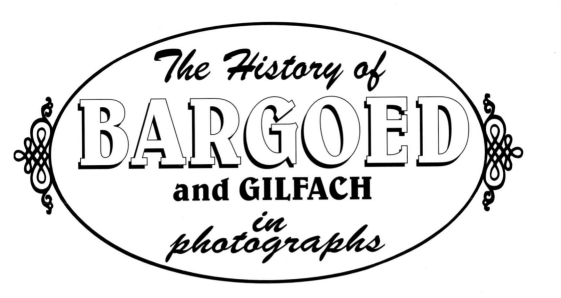

The History of BARGOED and GILFACH in photographs

Paul James

Foreword by
Councillor Harry A. Andrews, J.P.

Volume 2

Old Bakehouse Publications

Abertillery

First published in December 1998

ISBN 1 874538 07 7

Published in the U.K. by
Old Bakehouse Publications
Church Street,
Abertillery, Gwent NP3 lEA
Telephone: 01495 212600 Fax: 01495 216222

Made and printed in the UK
by J.R. Davies (Printers) Ltd.

Foreword

by Councillor Harry A. Andrews, J.P.

In whatever field of life it may happen, the inevitable consequences of success is the unremitting demand for a repeat performance.

As a result of the immense popularity of Volume One of Bargoed and Gilfach in Photographs, Paul James found himself under pressure from an appreciative public to delve into his comprehensive collection and compile another photographic history of the district. This was to take countless hours of dedication, and two years later this edition was completed. Sequels rarely have the impact of the original production, but I feel sure you will judge this volume to be just as interesting and informative as the previous book.

Encapsulated in the pages of both books is a proud history embracing more than a century. They will remind present and future generations of the constructive influence of this once thriving coal-mining community.

At the time of writing, plans are well advanced to bring about improvements that will raise the quality of our environment and provide an identity that our community will be proud of. As we prepare to enter the new Millenium,what the next one hundred years will achieve is open to conjecture. At the very least we will have the consolation of looking back on an interesting and proud history.

The author Paul James, has indicated that this book is his final endeavour and I believe therefore that we all owe him a debt of gratitude for providing us with the opportunity to relive those halcyon days of Bargoed and Gilfach.

Harry A Andrews.

Contents

FOREWORD

INTRODUCTION

CHAPTER 1   BARGOED TOWN & GILFACH

CHAPTER 2   ENTERTAINMENT & LEISURE

CHAPTER 3   LOCAL PEOPLE & EVENTS

CHAPTER 4   BUSINESS & INDUSTRIAL LIFE

CHAPTER 5   CHURCHES & CHAPELS

CHAPTER 6   SCHOOLDAYS

CHAPTER 7   SPORTING MEMORIES

Introduction

Upon publication of Volume One in this series of books, I was a little apprehensive as to how receptive the public might be, to what was ostensibly a book of photographs relating to Bargoed and Gilfach and the local inhabitants. Fortunately it was met with great enthusiasm, with the inevitable question "When will you be doing another?".

What was interesting, was to learn of the widespread circulation of the book. Former Bargoed and Gilfach residents appear to have travelled far and wide, seeking their fortunes and a new way of life during some previous difficult economic times. This is evidenced by Volume One having been despatched to numerous addresses scattered around the United Kingdom. Further afield, copies have reached Tasmania, New Zealand, the USA and Canada, attracting the eye of many ex patriots.

The collection of photographs in this latest volume offers further insight into our town and its people. For the younger element, there are strong reminders of the town's once thriving coal industry, with the plentiful employment and source of income that it used to provide. Those youngsters nowadays, will be fascinated and intrigued by an underground visit to a former working colliery and now have to pay for the privilege. Their fathers and grandfathers usually had little choice in the matter but to work hundreds of feet below ground to earn their living. Included in this book is a wide selection of other photographs which will draw attention to a disappearing past, such as latter-day enthusiasm for the church and chapel. These were once places at the centre of community life for many. Also to be considered are the numbers of old shops and premises now gone and replaced by something completely different. The familiar faces to be remembered on many of the pictures are always alluring and I have taken the liberty of including as many as possible to satisfy that demand.

I hope therefore that all who read this latest volume, will approve of its content and I would like to take the opportunity to thank those who kindly loaned their photographic treasures to help make the book possible.

Finally, my thanks must again go to Mr. Harry Andrews who agreed to provide the essential forewords for Volumes One and Two.

Paul James

CHAPTER 1

Bargoed Town & Gilfach

1. An aerial view of Bargoed from the earliest days of photography from the skies. The period is the early 1920s and looking at the bottom left-hand corner, it can be seen that the open-air baths have yet to be built in Bargoed Park.

2. Hanbury Square as seen during the 1950s, days when a double decked bus would stop here. The old wooden bus shelter is on the left, which was later to be dismantled and moved to the park. There are a few more familiar buildings to be remembered also, such as the Hanbury Cafe, owned by Pete Berzolla and Brinley Davies's cake shop. On the right was Lewis's the chemists, The Gem sweet shop and Ruthers for fruit and veg.

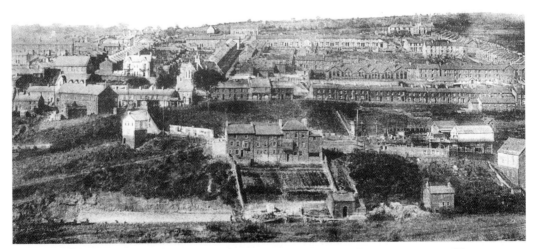

3. The collection of views of old Bargoed in this book span many years. The scene above is from around 1895 and looking from Aberbargoed, it can be seen that the Emporium has yet to be built and also St. Gwlady's Council School, which did not arrive until 1907.

4. The most prominent and most photographed building in the centre of the town at one time was the Emporium, where shoppers could buy almost anything for the home. This type of shop could not survive in Bargoed these days and this picture is from a bustling period during the 1920s. To the left is the former Calfaria Chapel, since demolished.

5. Early days in Hanbury Road and this view shows where the town's Post Office once stood. It is the building on the centre right of the photograph, the scene captured by the celebrated Cardiff photographer Ernest Bush.

6. It is the mid 1930s and looking up Wood Street, on the left is an antiquated bus, a Leyland Bull awaiting departure to Markham. A few more landmarks of days gone by include the War Memorial and on the opposite side, the Hanbury Cinema and Post Office.

7. The 1950s this time and a look at Hanbury Square, formerly referred to as Trafalgar Square. Note also an old First Aid box which used to be a familiar sight on the square.

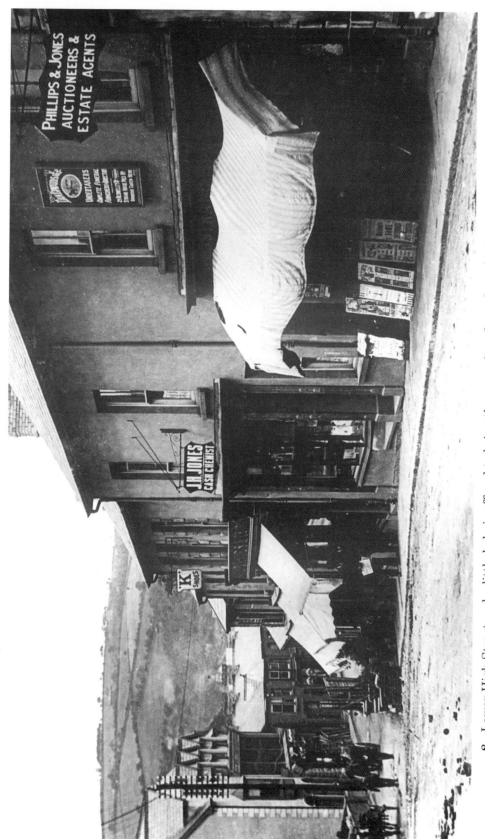

8. Lower High Street and a little help is offered to bring the scene into focus for today's population. On the left will now be found the Kwik Save store. This original photograph dates from about 1898, prior to the construction of the Palace Cinema.

9. The former Co-operative Stores are pictured on the left in Hanbury Road. Nearby is the town's Police Court, which after very many years is currently facing closure. The cost of the building incidently was a huge sum for the period, some £2300 and the court held its first session in December 1911.

10. This view is exceptionally old and is looking up the lower end of High Street in about 1895. The two cottages in the rear centre were demolished in about 1899 to make way for the construction of the Emporium.

11. The McDonnell Hotel at the corner of St. Gwlady's Avenue and McDonnell Road. The accompanying advertisement is much older than the photograph, as it offers fine stabling accommodation and one of the earliest telephone numbers in the town, Bargoed 7!

12. The residents of John Street in Bargoed will note a few improvements since this early 1900s view. The houses would probably have been quite new, as the road has yet to be surfaced and the railings on the right are still to appear.

13./14.   Two contrasting views, one distant and one close up of Bargoed Viaduct. Above, the scene is from the industrious 1930s and below, from the 1940s, the view is as it appeared before the new road was built to the right, beneath the arch.

15. A good view of the viaduct with three different railway tracks to be seen. Bottom left are the mountainous Rhymney, Brecon and Merthyr lines towards Fochriw. The Rhymney lines run over the viaduct and on the upper right are the lines owned by the Brecon and Merthyr Railway; these carrying the trains through New Tredegar and onwards to Rhymney. Also seen on this photograph are the quarries that once worked on the Aberbargoed side of the valley. On the bridge to the left is the old Trip Road, a route which is now overgrown.

16. Another very early view of the viaduct, one of the town's few remaining landmarks.

14

17. This is probably the oldest photograph in the book, as it is thought to date back to the 1870s. On the left is the original Old Mill Inn, the Old Mill Hotel has yet to be built. This was the site of an old corn mill which had been grinding grain since the 15th century. Its power was derived from the flow of the Darren and Rhymney rivers, the mill being renowned throughout the county for production of high quality roasted oatmeal.

18. The original picture postcard of this scene states the building to be 'A Country Residence near Bargoed'. Duffryn House, or the Puzzle House, is still there although it is pictured here in about 1920 before the road diversion in 1934.

19. This picture is from the beginning of the twentieth century, looking towards Hanbury Road. It pre-dates the construction of a number of buildings on the left such as the Hanbury Cafe. Centre left from the stream is a culvert which used to pass under the road. The marchers seen here are members of the local Baptist community.

20. Trafalgar Square before the much-changed appearance of today. There are some 1950s design Gelligaer buses parked outside the Hanbury Cinema and the Post Office. On the opposite side of the square the town's library has yet to be built.

21. Cardiff Road and Ruth Street and this is how these highways looked in about 1910. Two prominent buildings yet to appear are the Workmen's Institute and Trinity Chapel.

22. Hardly a valley town would be without its Workingmen's Institute in years gone by. Funded entirely by donation and voluntary help from the workers of the district, the building would be the centre of leisure activities and a library full of books. The historic building seen above was built in 1913 on land near the old Gilfach Fargoed Farm, Cardiff Road; costing some £5000 to complete, it was a huge financial responsibility for the workmen of the day.

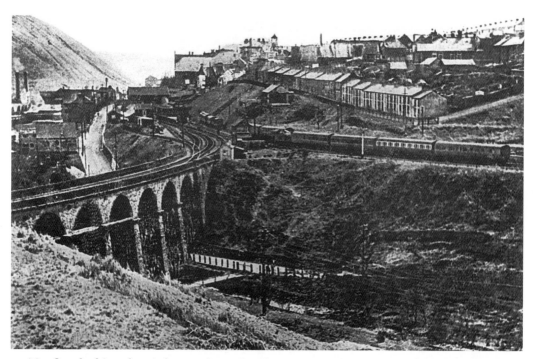

23. Overlooking the viaduct and town, to be seen is a clear view of the end of Bristol Terrace. This has since been demolished and the land converted into a car parking area.

24./25. Two photographs from the past showing views of the Old Mill Hotel. The former hump-backed bridge is seen above which used to lead into Bridge Street, the river nowadays being covered by a new road. The picture below is looking down Bridge Street with the hotel on the left and the original Old Mill Inn on the right; the photograph dates from about 1910.

26. One of the town's entrepreneurs during the earlier years of the twentieth century was Mr. Horace Davies. He was responsible for the construction of a number of fine buildings in the district, such as Oakland Hall, Bargoed Hall, The Junction Hotel and The Emporium. Mr. Davies is seen in the above photograph with his family at Bargoed Hall in 1910, the residence having been built in 1907.

27. A scene of opulence at a garden party held at Bargoed Hall in about 1917. This was a period at the height of the First World War and the event pictured here, was held by the British Red Cross Society to raise funds for their cause and to aid the war-wounded.

28. Bargoed Hall in Cardiff Road, the former residence of the Davies family. The photograph above is quite early, prior to some extensions having been added to the right of the building as seen in the lower picture. A modern-day medical surgery has now been erected to the left-hand side.

29. Bargoed Hall in about 1920. As will be noticed, the building has now been extended to the right and used as a surgery by Dr. Thomas Edward Richards, the father of Dr. Arthur Richards.

30. On the left is another reminder of Bargoed's one-time assortment of fine shops. This is the Bon Marché, first opened in the early 1900s. In 1912 it was acquired by Mr. Evan Davies who completely refurbished the building, modelling it on Cardiff's leading store David Morgan Ltd. Critics and shoppers at the time claimed there was no need to travel to Cardiff anymore for quality shopping, Cardiff had now come to Bargoed. Today this building is occupied by a branch of Burtons.

31. The photographer has captured the attention of a few bystanders in Hanbury Road in about 1896. Note that the left-hand side of the road is still lined with trees and awaits further development.

32. Upper High Street in the early 1920s when motor transport was beginning to make its presence felt in the town. The leading car is parked outside buildings which were later to become a Woolworth store, now developed as a car park.

33. This picture of High Street dates from 1951 and shows on the left, The Royal Hotel. This hotel was demolished in the 1960s to make way for a superstore. To the right some readers may well remember also the wallpaper shop and the Pontypridd Furnishing Co.

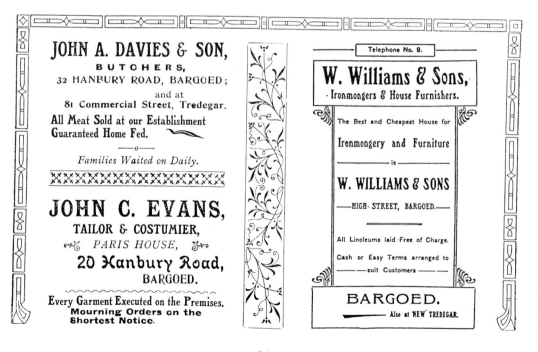

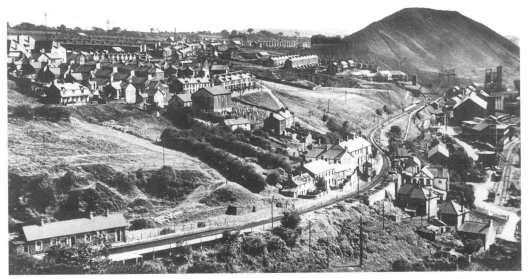

34. This view of Bargoed from the 1950s shows the waste tip and the colliery on the right with a branch line belonging to the Brecon and Merthyr Railway passing alongside. There are a few buildings seen here which are no longer, such as the Greyhound Inn, the Smith's Hotel and Aberbargoed station.

35. High Street in about 1951 and there are a number of familiar sights to be remembered by many. On the left is the Hall Cinema, directly opposite the Palace Cinema. A few more include Roath Furnishing, George, Rees and Jones and the National Assistance Office.

36. Hanbury Road which was in urgent need of improvement in about 1898. The 'Horse-less' carriage has yet to arrive, hence a rather poor road surface and some stepping stones leading to the house entrances. It was not an uncommon sight to see open drainage along the streets during these times. On the left is one of the town's earliest banks, The London Provincial.

37. Further along the road in about 1910 and there is a 'Grand Sale' in progress at Messers Powell and Jones's Bon Marché shop.

38. A view of Cross Street Gilfach probably taken during the 1940s. Stood in front of the now-removed waste tip is Mr. Jenkins who is on one of his insurance collecting rounds.

39. St. Mary Street and the corner of St. Anne's Crescent Gilfach. This photograph from around the 1920s shows further evidence of the coal waste tips that were once a common sight. The tip seen here was cleared in the late 1940s and now forms a park and recreation area.

40. This is a further picture allowing the reader to recall the progress that has been made in recovering what was once pure waste land. The view seen opposite looks towards Park Place from the corner of Aeron Place in about 1949. On the right is Mr. Glyn Harris, a Council foreman accompanied by one of his workers.

41. East View as it awaits the construction of a suitable road surface during the mid 1930s.

42. Heolddu Uchaf Farm near the Golf Club, pictured in 1885. The owner at the time was Mr. Lewis Jenkins who is seen resting on the railings. Also in the picture are, left to right - Jane (The Maid), Lalla (a cousin), Lewis Harris (Manservant) and a farm boy. Mr. Lewis Jenkins was the grandfather of the present owner Mr. Lydric Jenkins.

43. The ancient cottage which once stood in Angel Lane. There is nowadays no remaining evidence of this dwelling, the site having been completely landscaped.

Siencyn Morgan, The Welsh Hermit, Who has lived in the hut 20 years.

44. Mr. Siencyn Morgan who was something of a local celebrity many years ago. Mr. Morgan was a local man who refused to accept the luxuries of four walls and a roof over his head in the normal sense. He took it upon himself to live the life of a hermit, and lived in his shack seen here near Heolddu Uchaf Farm. Picture Postcards were published around the country presenting him as 'The Welsh Hermit'.

45. A final look at some of the former well-stocked shops of Hanbury Road as they stood in the early 1950s.

46. A general view of the town during the 1960s. On the right is the Junction Hotel and the old gasometer which was used to store coal-produced gas before natural supplies came from beneath the North Sea. Some other landmarks include the Royal Hotel and in the background, the once-familiar colliery coolers.

47. An exceptionally early picture of the Pier Head which shows Upper and Lower High Street in the early 1890s. Then came the period of major redevelopment with firstly, the cottages in the centre being demolished to make way for the Emporium and then, a little later, the adjacent houses came down to allow building of the Palace Cinema in 1907.

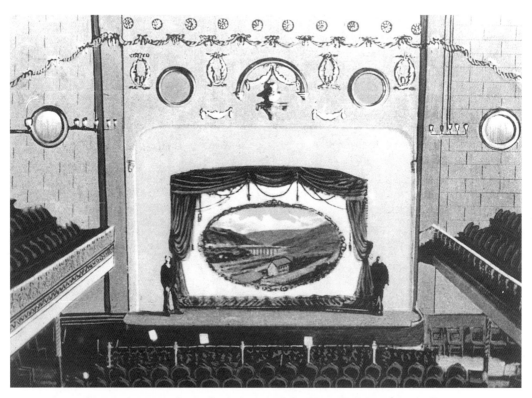

48. An early interior view from the balcony of the New Hall Playhouse. Built in 1907, it was later converted into a cinema, eventually being destroyed by fire in 1958. This site is now occupied by the Woolworth store.

CHAPTER 2

Entertainment & Leisure

49. The New Hall Playhouse and Cinema which was a source of entertainment for fifty years. The lower part of the building housed The Café Ballroom and also, as seen here on the right was Berni's Café and Temperance Bar.

50. Appropriately parked outside Mr. Miles the hairdresser's in the 1920s is this carnival float from Greenfield Street. The chosen topic is 'Sweeney Todd the Demon Barber'.

51. Another carnival lorry from Greenfield Street when the theme was 'Old and New'. Taken at the rear of the old open-air baths, the photograph includes - Mr. Ted Powell, Mrs. Evans, Yandell Powell, Dennis Brown. On the lorry are Mrs. Williams (old lady with shawl), Mrs. Treble (with specs), Mr. Dunn (far left), Anthony and Valerie Dunn (children).

52. The celebrations continue at Greenfield Street and this time it's May Day during the 1950s. Among those to be seen are Trevor Morgan, Mrs. Vano Smith, Diane Smith, John Jones, Maureen Collins, Anthony Dunn and Valerie Dunn.

53. The 1952 May Day carnival float of Greenfield Street seen at Bargoed Park, depicting countries of the world. Some of the entrants are Joan Smith, Carole Smith, Pam Smith, Irene Collins, Valerie Dunn, Edna Rees, Mrs. Mudge (Britannia), Vano Davies (Chinese) and Mrs. Morris.

54. An East View carnival from 1937 with the former Bargoed Colliery in the background. Accompanying the children are two ladies holding bunches of flowers who were proud to be the two eldest residents of the street at the time, they are Mrs. Lovett and Mrs. G. Morgan. Among the youngsters are Arona Llewellyn, Betty Evans, Marjorie Evans, Nellie Harrington, Kathleen Woods, Myrtle, Olga and Odelia McIvor.

55. A Greenfield Street party to celebrate VE Day in 1945. Among the many guests are the following - Harry Crocker, James Powell, Margaret Powell, Mrs. Dibbins, Mrs. Powell, Mr. Jones, Bill Smith, Mr. and Mrs. Charles, Mr. Williams, Mair Jones, Mr. Smally, Bert Mills, Mr. Johns, Hiram Johns, Billy Johns, Olive Powell and Gwyneth Davies.

56. The lucky residents of South Street Bargoed ready for a day trip to Barry Island in 1946, travelling in one of Charles Jenkins's coaches. The building just behind the bus was once the workshop of D.J. Thomas the undertaker. Among the passengers are Neville Lewis, Marion Overton, Sally Williams, Benny Williams, Clive Strange, June Gulliford, Pam Berrington, Olga Berrington, June Griffiths, Leighton Harris, Eddie Berrington, Sybil Berrington, Herbert Jones, Mrs. Lewis (holding the baby), Mrs. Wagstaff, Mrs. Greenaway, Mrs. Griffiths, Mrs. Williams, Mrs. Lovell, Mrs. Strange, Mrs. Davies, Mr. and Mrs. Charles Jenkins.

57. VE Day 1945, this time in Cross Street Bargoed. Some of those known at the party are - Mr. Taswell, Mrs. Smalley, Mr. Walkley, J. Lacey, J. Weaver, Mrs. Mudge, Mrs. M. Powell, Mrs. B. Jones, Eira Phillips, M. Weaver, John Richards, Roger Powell, Glyn Richards, John Roberts, Danny Powell, Idris Richards, Howard Roberts, Betty Walkley and Mavis Smalley.

58. From the 1930s a photograph of three brothers who formed the Mills family band. The band was known as Alberta and The Serenaders and left to right they are - Bert, Sid and Leonard. Bert was later to form another band known as The Invictor Dance Band.

59. Three members of the Gilfach Page Boys Jazz Band in 1938. Left to right are Ron Goodwin (New Tredegar), Harold Trivett (bass drumer of Gilfach) and Arthur Boilan (Aberbargoed).

60. The Gilfach Triangle Motor Cycle Club at their annual fancy dress and tramp supper held at the Capel Hotel. Some faces include Mr. J. Rosser, Mr. J. Cuttliffe, Mr. G. Sloggett, Mr. W. S. Price, Mr. R. Packer, Mr. S.V. Holloway, Mr. C.J. Bills, Mr. C. Summers, Mrs. K. Bowen, Mrs. K. Owen, Mr. E.J. Owen, Mrs. Packer, Mrs. F. Lerwill, Mr. W. Cook, Mr. W.H. Lerwill, G.L. Bowen, Mr. H. Brown, Mr. R.S. Holloway and Mr. Z. Bills.

61. The children here would now be in their 'thirties' so hopefully a few of them are reading this book. The scene is St. David's Day at Thomas Street Gilfach. Those to be seen include David Faulkener, Barry Faulkener, Wendy Davies, Julie Mayo, Lyn Waters, Janice Shaw, Lynda Shaw, Tracy Faulkener, Tina Gardener, Mrs Olga Langford, Alma Harris, Deana Hancox, Brian Jones, Carl Langford, Andrew Lewis, Alan Faulkener and Donna Hancox.

62. An Easter Bonnet Parade by the ladies' section at Gilfach Workmen's Club in the 1970s. Present are, left to right, back row - Alice Ennis, Maud Brown, Cora Jones, Beat Bolton, Pam Challenger, Ann Jones, Megan Lynch, Phyllis Yeo and Eileen Chard. Front: Jane James, Brenda Fox, Val Evans, Diane Davies, Marion Wright, May Watkins, Eric Stevens and John Goldsworthy.

63. Some members of Gilfach YMCA at a 1950 camp. Included in the picture are Glyn Morgan, Ernie Crick, Len Jones, Mrs. Flew, Kyrien Thomas, Graham Moore (Welsh International footballer), Alan Jarman, Gareth Williams and Stan Evans.

64. A fancy-dress party at Gilfach YMCA in 1942. The ladies' committee in the background include Mrs. Mag Davies, Mrs. Murray, Mrs. McGrath, Katie Matthews, Mrs. Riden, Margaret Lewis, Violet Hughes, Mrs. Jones, Mrs. Cooper, Joyce Jones, Mrs. Meadon, Beattie Davies (Art Shop), and Mr. T.G. Jones (Newsagent).

65. An annual event for many is a trip to Blackpool. This one from Plasnewydd Street (now St. Gwlady's Avenue) took place in 1953 and was organised by Mrs. Ridgeway and May Hughes. Here are a few names to remember - Mrs. Rachel Cleary, Mr. and Mrs. Morgan (Maypole), Teg Jones, Clarice Boyd, Margaret Cleary, Arthur Walters, Mr. and Mrs. Johns, Bill Powell, Bill Cleary, Mrs. Hathaway, Billy Osmond, Mrs. Osbourne, Dennis Pitt, Elvet Foster, Ianto Roberts, May Hughes, Mrs. Ridgeway and Mrs. Thomas (The Shop).

66. The Bargoed Girls Youth Choir in 1949 which was comprised of girls from Bargoed and Hengoed schools. Some names are known and they are - Iowerth Thomas (Leader), Margaret Hughes (Pianist), Mr. Lewis, Marina Evans, Valerie Harding, Marion Davies, Corine Edwards, Marina Perks, Margaret Evans, Eira Dare, Beryl Hughes, Rita Rowlands, Margaret Bowen, Kathleen Brookes, Myrtle Meadon, Enid Rees, Margaret Rees, Brenda Evans and Marlene Hughes.

67. The Bargoed Philarmonic Choral Society in 1946 with conductor Mr. Teddy Jenkins. Also to be seen are - Mr. J. Carter, Mr. J. Box, Mr. R. Owen, Mr. L. Davies, Mr. and Mrs. L. Lambert, Mrs. C. Box, Mrs. G. Jenkins, Mrs. D. Lloyd-Jones, Mrs. J. Harris, Mrs. P. Owen, Mr. G. Owen, Mr. A. Jones, Mrs. Saunders and Mrs. F. Thomas.

68. The Bargoed Male Voice Choir posing for a photograph in 1969. With them in the front row are Cliff Horrell (Musical Director), Mr. Fred Evans M.P. (President) and Mr. Jack Harris (Chairman).

69. The Emporium Staff Dance 1954. There are many faces to be seen which include manager Mr. Ford and Mrs. Ford, Mr. and Mrs. Cook (Gown Shop), Mr. Graham Price (Window Dresser), Ken Lewis, Miss D. Smith, Miss G. Moore, Miss T. Clavin, Miss Jean Jones and Miss Lilian Davies.

70. Another group of fine entertainers from the past, The McDonnell Ladies Choir. The photograph was taken in St. Gwlady's Church Hall during the 1950s. Among the group are Mrs. Ada Meadon (Soloist), Mr. Williams, Iris Osbourne, Tom Evans (Comedian), Florrie Thomas, Joyce King, Muriel Evans (Conductor), W. Boobyer (Accompanist), Mr. James, Mrs. Morris, Beryl Noonan and Mrs. Elad.

71. The Gilfach Amateur Players Volunteer Charity Group in 1983 and they are - May Ashton, Edith Young, Muriel Rees, Judith Rees, Lily Jones, Olga Williams, Joan Thompson, Norma Lewis, Melita Churchouse, Frances Lynch, Sheila Heath, Alan Dando, Glenys Lippiatt, Shelly Meadon, Pat Walters, Robert Evans (Soloist), Maureen Corbin (Pianist) and Debbie Romais.

CHAPTER 3

Local People & Events

72. During wartime it was necessary for the ladies to adapt to the jobs normally carried out by men who were then on active service; a fine job was done too! Here are members of The National Fire Service Bargoed in 1942 with left to right, Mrs. C. Box, Miss J. Williams, Miss O. Williams, Mr. D.O. Hay (Divisional Officer), Mrs. Golding, Mrs. M. Atkins and Miss Beryl Jones.

73. Another noble organisation, The Women's Voluntary Service pictured outside Cartref in 1960. Amongst the group are Mrs. Alice Lanford, Mrs. Gwladys Jones, Mrs. Lloyd, Mrs. Jenny Jenkins (The Bank), Mrs. Smith, Elizabeth Howells, Betty Fox, Phyllis Owen and Mrs. Archard.

74. The St. John Ambulance Brigade in 1966 and to be noted left to right are, Back Row: J.H. Jones, Mrs. E. Howells, Miss L. Chilton, Mr. S. James, Mrs. C. Tomkinson and Mr. Idris Jones (Brithdir). Front: Miss J. Evans, Mrs. J. Jones, Miss Evans, Mrs. P.H. Ford and Mrs. G. Bruton.

75. The ladies of Bargoed Town Women's Guild in 1957 and many of their names can be recalled as follows - Mrs. Jones, Mrs. Lewis, Miss Morris, Mrs. May James, Mrs. Llewellyn, Mrs. Luther, Mrs. Beryl Noonan, Mrs. Griffiths, Mrs. Peggy Lewis, Mrs. Joyce Jones, Mrs. Olivia Bowen, Mrs. Margaret Maddox, Mrs. Mair Jones, Mrs. Dilys Davies, Mrs. Ada Meadon, Mrs. Alice McCarthy, Mrs. Muriel Evans and Mrs. Williams.

76. Nine young ladies pose for this photograph at the top of West Street during the Coronation celebrations of June 1953. They are Celia Grist, Jackie Davies, Catherine Grist, Diane Williams, Olive Boswell, Priscilla Francis, Irene Protheroe, Julie Brass and Nita Brass.

77. A Concert scene at St. Margaret's Church Hall Gilfach in the 1940s. The musicians in the front are Mrs. Ploughman (Pianist), Dick Horton, Arthur Barnett, Charlie Pratten (Violinists) and Harold Trivett (Drums). Some other faces to recall are Ron Morgan, Remo Morgan, Meredith Rees (Curate), Jack Mullet, Olga Morgan, Peter Ridley, Wilf Bartlett, Alan Dando, Everet Ploughman, Mr. and Mrs. Duke, Iris Beer, Miss Moss, Joyce Evans, Cyril Price, Peggy Baines, Brenda Pratten and Florrie Pratten.

78. The Bargoed Cambrian Gleemen at Bargoed Hall in 1947 and reading left to right they include - Back: J. Edwards, J. Maidment, J. Jones, H. Stephens, G. Yeoman, T. Jones, E. Price, H. Bromham, W.J. Holyfield, R.J. Bromham and J. Rees. Third Row: R. Major, T. Carter, E. Maund, H. Richards, W. Richards, E. Morgan, J. Howells, C. Evans, F. Gardiner, G. Morgan and J. Carter. Second Row: E. Davies, D. Lewis, G. Hughes, Joyce Mullett, D. Jones, Mavis Rowlands, P.H. Ford, W. Madley and B. Williams. Front: J. Carter, D. Daniels and A. Dando.

79. On the left is Mr. Brian Rogers, Chairman of Caerphilly Borough Council with Councillor Harry Andrews on the far right. In the centre is Dr. Daffyd Rhys Williams of the Canadian Space Agency who visited Bargoed in August 1998 and whose town connections are described on page 70. During his flight aboard the Space Shuttle Columbia Dafydd had carried with him a number of items of Welsh interest and researching his family tree, particularly concerning his mother's side in the Bargoed area has become just another of his pastimes.

80. A presentation is being made to Mr. John Evans, Clerk to the Council on his retirement in 1943. Photographed outside the G.U.D.C. Electricity Dept. in Hanbury Road, Nurse Morgan hands over a gift. Among those also present are V. Fowler, Miss L. Chilton, T. Lewis, R. Williams (Accountant), Mary Curnach, E. Evans (Valuation Officer), A.S. Williams J.P., Mary Morgan (Health Visitor), G. Warlock, D. Davies, Mr. Downs, A. Williams, J.R. Hughes (Deputy Clerk), R. Morgan, Mr. Rowlands and F. Hill.

81. A solemn scene at Park Place Gilfach during the funeral of Mr. Leonard Wilkinson in 1953. Aged just 24 years, Mr. Wilkinson was tragically electrocuted in an accident at Gilfach Jazz Band hut at the rear of the YMCA. The procession is led by Mr. John James (Sec.) and Mr. Harding (Treasurer) with the Red Paraders Jazz Band.

82. Some local personalities from the 1950s relaxing at The Top Hat Club. To be seen are J.S. Turner (Doctor), Jack David (Landlord at the Ivor Arms), Tom White (Mining Engineer), Fred Lucas (Butcher), David Sallis (Ironmonger), George Maddox, Edgar Bowen (Lloyds Bank) and Trevor Rees (George, Rees and Jones' shop).

83. This is a photograph of some Gilfach pals taken in Church Fields in 1944. Sat at the front is Bill Lerwill, one of the very few people who had a camera and film in wartime; it was his time operated camera that took this picture. Also included are Denny Rowlands, Joe Stuckey, Doreen Faulkener, Simon Stuckey and Sid Faulkener.

84. Bargoed and the surrounding district is not short of heroes from the past. On the left is 1284419 Edgar James Matthews of 17 Maesygraig Street Gilfach posing in his RAF wireless-operator attire. Sadly this young man was killed during the height of World War Two on August 3rd 1941 aged just 19 years.

In Loving Memory

OF

A.B. WILLIAM THOMAS DAVIES,

Drake Battalion, 1st Royal Naval Brigade.

The Beloved Son of Mr. & Mrs. D. DAVIES.

OF 3, MAESYGRAIG STREET, GILFACH, BARGOED.

Died from wounds on December 22nd, 1915, received whilst serving with the Mediterranean Force at the Dardanelles.

AGED 19 YEARS.

"And by it he being dead yet speaketh."—HEBREWS, XI., 4

85. Trafalgar Square Bargoed in about 1917. A relatively new weapon, the Tank is seen attracting the crowds as part of the nationwide campaign to sell War Bonds to help finance the First World War. The message on the banner reads 'Better British Bonds than Prussian Bondage'. This was the stirring call for patriotism during the period.

86. General Election Day 1921 and members of the local Independent Labour Party pose for the cameraman outside Tattenham Corner Shop at the bottom of Heolddu Road, and the corner of Francis Street. Shop-owner Mrs. Pope is standing just off the centre holding baby Lesley.

87. These gentlemen, calling themselves the Bargoed Pals Outing Club are pictured in the park in 1918 and include the following. Back: A. Hamer, J. Matthews, E. Harris, J. Quick, R. Llewellyn, J. Griffiths, W. Bevan, G. Cox, A. Kedward, E. Morgans, W. Thomas, E. Jones and A. Simmonds. Middle Row: G. Bolton, S. Woodward, Miss Alethea Aubrey, W. Williams, W. Woodward, W. Pugh, W.R. Maddocks, Miss E.J. Langdon, F. Duggan and H. Bosanko. Front: Unknown, Mr. Innes, B. Ripley, J. Davies, S. Burnett, D. Carpenter, M. Chowles, J. Cook and A. Robinson.

88. A Gilfach carnival float celebrating The Festival of Britain in 1951. The ladies seen from the left are: Hazel Thompson, Christine Rice, June Bidgway, Eirwen Williams, Melita Davies, Eveline Turner (Mrs Gilfach) and Marlene Brock (Miss Gilfach).

89. Another source of youth entertainment was the Aberbargoed Roller Skating Club run by Mr. Lionel Hall, their trainer. The boys and girls are pictured here at Gilfach YMCA in March 1980 and left to right are - Back: Belinda Grimshaw, Alyson Hurst, Wendy Lippiett, Susan Lewis, Michelle Wilmott, Mandy Lippiett, Denise Carey and Anthony Wilmott. Front: Maria Jones, Jacqueline James, Martyn Hurst, Debbie Romais, Debbie Knight and Mandy Harris.

90. A photograph from about 1910 of an important but sad occasion. This is the funeral procession of Mr. Evan Thomas the local miners' agent. The scene is along Gilfach Street, near the Capel Hotel. Today a garage is to be seen on the right which was owned at one time by Mr. Stan Hughes.

91. Members of St. Gwlady's Church Cub Troop are seen here in 1958 or 1959. The young lads include - Back: ?, ?, ?, Jeff Willetts, Martin Meadon, Howard Strange, David Jones, Graham Rogers and Adrian Parry-Lewis. Middle: Howard Evans, David Price, Alan Morris, Ken Collins, Peter Collins, Ceri Morgan, Clive Jones, Gary Davies, Malcolm Pratten and Ronald Groves. Front: Lyndon Williams, Robert Buckland, Huw Williams, John Banks, David Dowling, and unknown.

92. Another 1953 Coronation Party, at Heolddu Drive on this occasion. Amongst the crowd are Mrs Yates, Mrs. Morgan, Bernice Hunter, Ethel Quick, Gwladys Evans, Valerie Evans, Sandra Sheen, Selwyn Quick, Howard Quick, Ray Clabby, Ann Price, Eunice Morgan, Margaret Price, Clive Jones, Wendy Walters, Brython Jones, Brian Davies, Fay Baker, Peter Price, John Baker and Howard Baker.

93. A thronging Trafalgar Square amidst a campaign for funds for the First World War. Just to the right of the trees can be seen some troops with a primitive Tank.

94. Following the building of the cenotaph in Whitehall London, towns and villages throughout the country asked for War Memorials to honour those lost in The Great War 1914-1918. Above is the scene at the unveiling of Bargoed's memorial at Trafalgar Square on May 31st 1918.

95. Bargoed Home Guard, 19 Glamorgan Battalion seen outside Bargoed Institute in 1941. Their leader was Mr. T.D. Evans who is sat in the centre of the front row.

96. A well known name in Gilfach is that of 'Walters' and here are members of the family in the 1930s. Standing are Lewis (Grocer), Tal (NUM Lodge Sec. and Councillor), Queenie, Bill,George (NUM Sec. and Councillor), Herbert (Sweet Shop). Seated are Richard (Dick Flagon, Drayman and Grocer), Anne (Nurse) and Margaret.

97. The great boxer of the 1930s and 1940s was Tommy Farr. Here is a party to wish him success in his fight in the USA against World Champion Joe Louis in 1937. Some of the well-wishers are Phil and Kitty Maher; Albert Morgan, Dewi Llewellyn, Kenny and Roy Burgess, Eileen O'Keefe, Olwyn Davies, Mary Davies, Lily Morgan, John Davies, Mair Lucas, Ruby Thomas, Lily Hill, Gwyneth Waite, Doreen Hall, Tommy Morgan, Billy Evans, Mr. Evans, Mary Hall, Lily Jones, Ivy and Elsie Huxley, Mrs. Francis, Mrs. Meadow, Mrs. Hill, Mrs. Burgess, Mr. Llewellyn, Mr. McIvor, Dai Matthews, Glyn Davies, Arthur Williams, Bill Hall, Bill Morgan, Malcolm Lucas, Billy Hill, Glyn Evans, Danny Evans, Nan Morgan, Marjorie Evans, Mrs. Stephens, Ken Hall, Charlie Westlake, Laura Thomas, Les Francis and Griff Jones.

98. Bargoed Boys' Brigade at their headquarters, the Wesleyan Chapel in Wood Street (The Lesser Hall) in 1952. Here are a few names for readers to recall - Roy Newall, Len Ford, Sid Bisp, Sid Bevan, Glyn Jenkins, Alan Howells, Terry Probyn, Bill Davies, Peter Rees, John Harry, Alan Button, Dai Edwards, Cameron Cox, Gerald Evans, Mr. Dean, Mr. Bellamy, Morris Jones (Captain), Rev. Bone, Mr. Gittings, Mr. Hill, Gwilym Williams, Tudor Jones, John Lloyd, John Hill and David Pearce.

99. The residents of Usk Road Bargoed celebrating The Festival of Britain in 1951. Amongst the many faces to be seen are Margaret Barnett, Bessie James, Emily Adams, Tommy Adams, Phyllis Jones, Margaret Jones, Gwen Smart, Jean Smart, Phyllis Lee, Annie Jenkins, Mrs. Jones, Mrs. Davies, Mrs. Edwards, Mrs. Griffiths, Haydn Griffiths, Mr. Roberts, Mrs. Day, Marjorie Jones, Clifford Smart, Elizabeth Vaughan, Graham Davies, Lyndon Vaughan, Susan Jones, Tudor Jones, Edward Vaughan, Marilyn Jones, Gloria Norman, Mary Jones, Ann Jones, David Griffiths, Clive Thomas, Alma Jones, John Jones, Billy Adams, Brian Edwards, Alan Jones, David Roberts, Glenys Coles and Lily Coles.

100. On the left is Mr. Phil Maher pictured with his trophies in 1955 as Bargoed's champion chrysanthemum grower. His success was measured at the annual show of the Bargoed and District Chrysanthemum Society when he took four cups, four medals, four certificates and the Blue Ribbon of the show.

101. Both of these faces will be remembered by many, they belonging to the late Alan Withers and his wife Eveline, formerly of Oakland Hall Bargoed. Both were local solicitors, Mrs. Withers starting her career with W.D. Robert Lewis and Co. and Mr. Withers working with Messers John Evans and Co. Amalgamation amongst Bargoed's solicitors resulted in the Withers practicing with the partnership of Hugh James, Jones and Jenkins until retirement; Mr. Withers in 1982 and his wife in 1988.

102. From the 1930s comes a picture of Gilfach's Ainon Baptist Church Sisterhood with an antiquated canvas-topped bus. Some of the members are Sarah Deneen, Mrs. John Rees, Nurse Lane, Miss D. Fisher, Miss P. Fisher, Howard Greenwood, Sarah Morris, Annie John, Amelia Rees and Lil Greenwood.

103. Members of Gilfach YMCA stopping for a photograph before setting off for a Welsh Football International. Back Row: Kyrien Thomas, Bert Chard, Harry Andrews, Peter Ridley, Tudor Davies, Peter Lewis, Ron Hancox, John Bayliss and Mel Mantle. Middle: David Phillips, Alan Jarman, Nona Clark, Brenig Jones, Eric Stephens and George Renton. Front: Lewis Bissex, Gerald Evans, Mr. Russell and Bryn Jones.

104. St. Anne's Street Gilfach marking the 1951 Festival. Some names to look for include Roy Davies, Eric Rogers, David Rice, Gary Rice, Clarice Rice, Eirwen Williams (The Street's Queen), Rose Smith, Gwladys Parry, Minnie Brookes, Mary Thompson, Pauline Lewis, Nancy Griffin, Les Thompson, Brian Williams, Ceridwen Bartlett, Gwyneth Bartlett, Dai Bartlett, Betty Thorley, Greta Jones, Trevor Jones, Sid Williams, Gareth Williams, Malcolm Parry, Mr. and Mrs. Eddie Davies, Ceridwen Evans, Carol Lewis and Mr. and Mrs. George King.

105. Mr. John Dines from East View is seen in 1947 on Gilfach show field at the rear of the Capel Hotel. Familiar scenery in the background shows the colliery workings and waste tip. Mr. Dines was to become a well known local builder in later years.

106. Another popular character from the past was Mr. Tommy John who lived at Maes-y-Graig Street Gilfach. To some he would be better known as Bobby John, he being a part-time Special Constable whilst also working at the colliery.

107. The challenging St. Anne's Street ladies football team seen here in about 1949 and the players include - Back: Irene Thompson, Gwyneth Rees, ?, Fred Thompson (Ref), Gwyneth Bartlett, Miss Rogers, Betty Boulton, Archie Thompson (Trainer), unknown. Middle: Rose Rogers, Joan Thompson, Clarice Rice, Audrey Roberts, Pauline Lewis. Front: Minnie Brookes, Miss Brookes, Eirwen Williams, Rose Smith, Margaret Boulton.

108. The year is 1978 and these are entrants from Maes-y-Graig Street dressed as a popular brand of chocolate biscuit for the carnival. Left to right are June Hurst, Pam Cannon, Jane James, Mair Ganderton, Irene Davies, Cheri Evans, Kay Davies, Marilyn Foster and Joan Wilmott. The children are Martyn Hurst, Sian Ganderton, Nicola Foster and Sarah Evans.

109. Members of the Hyndman family, former owners of Bargoed's oldest hotel, The Plasnewydd. Everyone played their part in running the business, Mr. Tom Hyndman being a keen boxing supporter, often held matches in the upper rooms of the hotel. Left to right are Back: Cissy Holloway, Rheola Phillips and Tom Hyndman. Front: Catherine Jones, Rosie Edwards, Sarah Hyndman, Tom Hyndman Snr., Ethel Quick and Sarah Grist.

110. From the 1940s this picture shows members of The Lennox Club Committee who are - Back: Jack Curtis, Mr. Boobyer (Undertaker), Illtyd Thomas. Middle: Mr. Vaughan, Will Clayton, Harry Williams, John Howells. Front: Tom Price, Harry Langford and Tom the steward.

111. The annual Emporium Staff Dinner and Dance which used to be a popular and well-attended function. On this occasion the year is 1948, the event being held at Bargoed Institute.

112. Members of The Capel Hotel Darts Team with their trophies. A few names are known including D. Roberts, E. Lewis, D. Bond, D. Pitt, S. Bryant, W. Bond, G. Thomas, J. Marsh, I. Morgan, I. Evans, C. Wilson, D. Heath, W. Nelmes, Mr. Jones, J.A. Jones, J. Goldsworthy, F. O'Keefe, Ernie Maund, Bill O'Keefe, Bill Bond and M. Huxley.

113. Some more members of the darts team at The Capel enjoying some refreshment and a game in 1954. Left to right are Cyril Watkins, Charlie Edwards, Denzil Davies and Billy Oliver. Sadly Cyril Watkins was killed in an accident at Bargoed Colliery in October 1954 aged just 29 years.

CHAPTER 4

Business & Industrial Life

114. The early Bargoed Post Office when it was situated at Number Two, Croft House Station Road. This photograph dates from the 1880s and shows the Postmaster of the time Mr. Edward Lewis, accompanied by the telegraph runner, postman and office staff.

115./116. Above is Mr. David Henry Evans holding his horse 'Daisy'; Mr. Evans being the manager for W.E. Vaughan and Co. the Dry Cleaners. The little girl on the photograph is his daughter Dyllis and the picture dates from the year 1916. The lower photograph shows the shop at 51 Hanbury Road where Mr. Evans resided. Stood outside in about 1920 are, on the left Miss Beale the manageress with assistant Ivy Evans holding baby sister Muriel.

117. The long established Cosy Corner confectioners and tobacconists which stood in lower High Street Bargoed. The tall lady stood in the doorway is Rebecca Evans.

118. Only the more mature-aged readers will remember and appreciate how convenient it was to have the groceries delivered to the door by horse and cart. The horse, a very intelligent animal, needed little guidance once the round was learned; the animal knowing where and when to stop automatically without having to be told by its master. Seen here is Mr. Warren Lewis of The Bird in Hand Bakery setting off for the Bargoed Show from the rear of Moorland Road in about 1912.

119. The displaying and marketing of fresh meat has attracted some criticism in recent years, not so in years gone by. The above scene is at the Hereford Butchers in Hanbury Road in 1910 and the young lad on the far right with his delivery basket is Mr. Will Churchouse.

120. This is the old ironmonger's shop of the Williams' in High Street, the premises now forming a branch of Kwiksave Supermarkets. This was a family-run business which was to have eventual connections far beyond Bargoed and Mother Earth itself. Many readers will recall during 1998, wide news coverage of Wales' claim to have at last, an astronaut of Welsh origins circling the earth. Dr. Dafydd Rhys Williams was the acclaimed man in space, his grandfather Alfred being involved in the family ironmongery business as seen in the photograph opposite in the early years of this century. Dafydd's father Bill, probably not too interested in continuing in the trade, and, as the country was in a great economic downturn, decided to emigrate to Canada in 1926; the Welsh descendant space traveller being born there in 1954. Dr. Williams visited Wales in August 1998, a photograph of the event appearing on page 48 of this book.

121. The staff of Woolworths posing for a photograph when the store was situated in Upper High Street. Many of the names have been traced as follows. Back: Audrey Bron, ?, Bessie Jones, ?, Lilian Davies, Mary Evans, Jessie Ann Davies, Jean Hodgkins, Joan Baker, Sheila Jones, Alan Owens and Roy Stevens. Third Row: Maureen Phillips, Jean Edwards, Marina Rees, Ruby Foster, Nancy Jones, ?, Joan Smith, ?, ?, Betty Gifford, Brenda Clapham, ?, ?. Second Row: Nina Munkley (Head Cashier), Myrtle Bowen (Supervisor), Lorna Evans, Gwladys Day (Manageress), George Cook (Manager), Jean Faulkener, Betty Fussell and Rona Edwards. Front: Doreen Powell, Eileen Davies, Mul Evans, Megan Nicholls, Olga Berrington and Marlene Turner.

122. The hairdressing salon of Idris and Hannah Lloyd which was in Hanbury Road; the two children on the doorstep are Ellen and Elfed Lloyd. The year is 1916 evidenced by the headlines on the news board reporting the trial of Sir Roger Casement who was later to be hanged for treason, during the period of World War One and the Irish troubles.

123. Mr. Gus Jones, a native of Pontypool who opened his first jewellery shop in Hanbury Road Bargoed in 1903. A popular figure and active in local organisations, he was the founder of the business which exists to this day with a number of branches throughout the valleys.

124. Mr. D.S. Jones who originally came from Merthyr Tydfil was proprietor of Davy's Shop which once stood in Bargoed's High Street. This was one of the first grocery stores to be started in the expanding town, being established in the year 1875. Like Mr. Gus Jones, David Jones too was active in many local affairs and known to be a strong businessman yet one who took a close personal interest in the welfare of his customers.

125. A picture of 'Davy's Shop' High Street as seen in 1909. The premises above belonged to Messers Phillips and Jones, the well known auctioneers and valuers. Davy's was one of the earliest grocery and provision merchants in the town and to understand the whereabouts of this old trader these days, on the left will be found Keith's Butchers, presently owned by Doug Hughes and a newsagent on the right.

126. From the 1950s when Bargoed Post Office was situated next to the Hanbury Cinema in Hanbury Square. Seated in the centre is Postmaster Mr. Joseph Kelk surrounded by his staff. The sorting office on the left is now a bakery and the Post Office has become a fruit and vegetable shop.

127. Another popular and well-known grocery chain throughout the valleys was Peglers. This type of grocery store was the usual such venue for the personal service and home delivery of one's shopping before the arrival of the American-style supermarkets in the 1960s. The shop seen here was in Hanbury Road and is pictured some 70 or 80 years ago.

128. This is how Albert Dickinson's Garage under Cardiff Road looked in 1921. Standing on the right is Mr. William Jones who started work as a driver despite serious injuries received in The Great War. Mr. Jones was shot in both legs at the devastating Battle of The Somme in France in 1916, on his nineteenth birthday. Ironically his pal was killed by the same bullet and Mr. Jones lay in a trench for three days before being rescued. These days the garage is the site of a car showroom.

129. Tattenham Corner Shop at the bottom of Heolddu Road, adjoining Francis Street. Stood at the main entrance on the right are William and Alethea Pope with their son Leslie. Mr. Ernest Pope is stood at the side entrance and the year is about 1923.

130. This is the original building occupied by Powell and Jones Bon Marché shop in Bargoed. During this period, in about 1904 the company was based in Abertillery hence the wording placed over the shop seen here. On offer are such antiquated things as 'Mantles and Millinery' (cloaks and hats in today's language). The building was later much enlarged and nowadays is partly occupied by a branch of Burtons.

131. Mr. Bill Pember seen on his rounds delivering groceries in Vere Street Gilfach. Bill worked at the Chinnock Family's shop at No.12 Vere Street and he is pictured here during the 1930s with his cart hauled by 'Mag' the faithful mare.

132. The winter of 1947 might be remembered by some as the last of the great winters to hit the country. This is the scene in Hanbury Road showing a few former shops such as The Home and Colonial, D. Sallis and Sons the ironmongers and J. Parfitt the tobacconists.

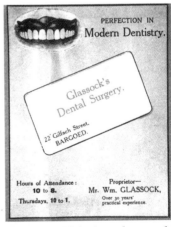

PERFECTION IN
Modern Dentistry.

Glassock's
Dental Surgery.

22 Gilfach Street.
BARGOED.

Hours of Attendance:
10 to 8.
Thursdays, **10 to 1.**

Proprietor—
Mr. Wm. GLASSOCK,
Over 30 years'
practical experience.

133. The old fruit and vegetable shop belonging to Ruthers in High Street. The photograph on the left belongs to the 1930s and shows Mary Knight on the left and Betty Jones on the right. It is always interesting to some readers as to where these former premises used to be; Ruther's will nowadays be better recognised as a branch of The Bradford and Bingley Building Society.

134. A gathering of some members of the local Licensed Victuallers Association in about 1950 and one or two familiar faces may be recognised - Will Bevan (The Old Mill), Bert Burgess (The Hanbury), Eddie Davies (The Baileys Deri), Edwin Davies (McDonnell), George Roberts (The Royal Hotel), Tom Hyndman (The Plasnewydd), Fred Owen (The Railway Caerphilly), Mr. and Mrs. Woods (The Wingfield Llanbradach) and Mr. Smart (The Half Way Pengam).

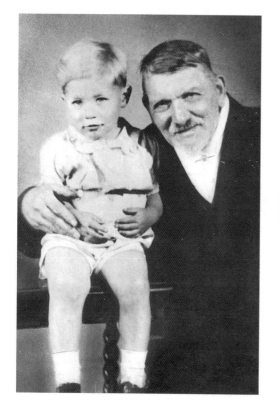

135. Some members of the Withers family, proprietors of the oldest Sunday Newspaper business in Bargoed. On the left is Mr. Rowland Withers with grandson Alan and on the right are Ivor and Ivy. The business originally started in West Street is now at Park Place Gilfach and still run by members of the family, Alan and Kath Withers.

136. Gelligaer Urban District Council commenced a local bus service on June 16th 1928. The first driver was Mr. Ron Brookes who is seen on the right of this picture accompanied by conductor John Davies. The bus is from the Leyland range of coaches, a 'Leyland Tiger' and the period is about 1929.

137. Following the end of the war in 1945, public transport returned to normality although fuel was to remain rationed for some time after. Seen here in the centre is Mrs. Tegwyn Evans who was the first bus conductress in peacetime in the Rhymney Valley. At the back is Jack Howells and in front are Cecil Davies and Bernard Williams.

138. A view of Bargoed Colliery in about 1910. In the background is a one-time, so familiar sight in the Welsh Valleys, the proverbial coal tip. On the right of the photograph is the power house.

139. Another general view of the colliery in 1912 which shows the washery on the left. Just in front of the washery is the Brithdir Pit, also to be known as Bargoed Housecoal and to the right are the North and South shafts.

140./141. The visitor to Bargoed today might find it difficult to appreciate just how industrious the town once was; both of these pictures from about 1912 confirm that fact. Above can be seen the by-products plant and below is the washery. The washery was constructed in 1905 for coal cleansing and as output soared, so the customers became more and more demanding and expected the cleanest possible fuel.

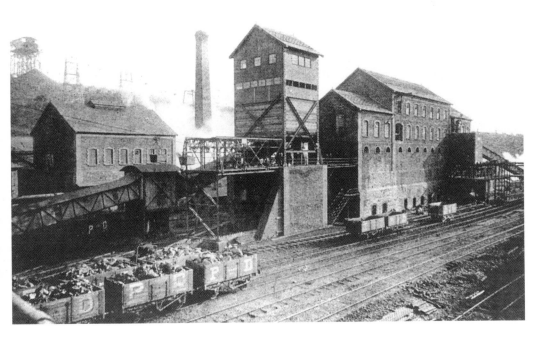

142. Men of the Bargoed Mines Rescue Brigade who were responsible for the saving of eighteen men at the great Senghenydd disaster near Pontypridd. That tragic event took place on October 13th 1913 and claimed the lives of 436 miners. The team in this picture consists of William (Job) Evans and Ben Rees at the back with Tom Griffiths, George Gregory, Charles Williams, W.T. Reynolds and Mr. C.M. Kitto (Superintendent).

143. Some of the tradesmen at the colliery in 1950 and looking left to right they are S. Barnett, B. Blow, R. Heath, D. Bennett, J. Foster, J. McCarthy, ?, L. Steed, Cyril Beale (Midge), G. Eynon, ?, ?.

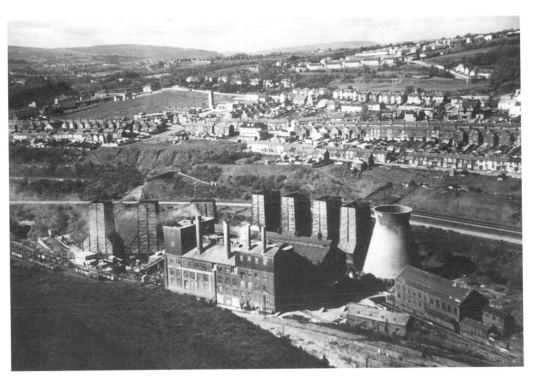

144./145. Two views of the colliery which show the extensive workings of the coolers and powerhouse. Mining operations began here in 1897, the undertaking belonging to the esteemed Powell Duffryn Company. What was to become a huge concern throughout the mining valleys of South Wales, the company was first formed by one Thomas Powell of The Gaer near Newport. His first venture was the purchase of a small colliery near Llanhilleth in the Ebbw Valley in about 1830. This early coal mine was worked by Powell with the help of two or three colleagues with their primitive picks and shovels.

146./147. Two additional colliery pictures, above from 1958 and below, about 1912 displaying the hive of activity that once was; these will be of particular interest to former workers here. Above, coal-laden trams are being conveyed up the creeper towards the screening process. Below is an interior view of the washery and the process involved in cleaning the extracted coal.

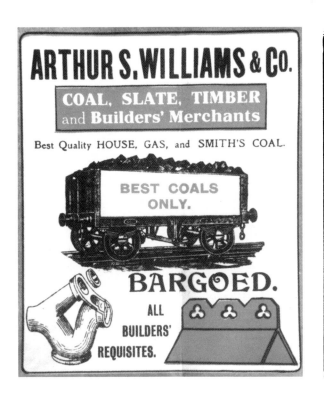
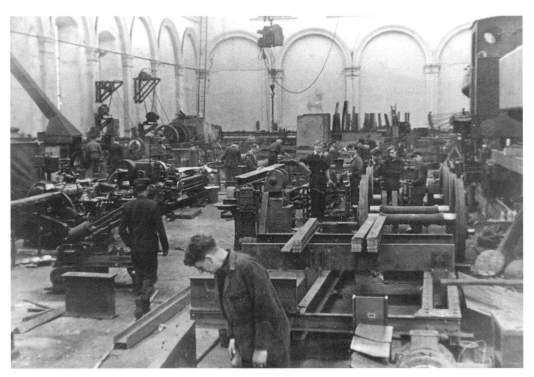

148. An interior view of the busy works at Bargoed Colliery in about 1950 and some of the men seen here are S. Jones, T. Cook, F. Jones, G. Steed, R. Heath, A. Campbell, R. Clifton, C. Neat, Mr. Griffiths, Mr. Stockwood and L.Brown.

149. The former colliery at Gilfach with its familiar chimney stack. In the background is another old landmark, the waste tip of Bargoed Pit. The year of this particular photograph is about 1915.

150. A steam wagon in operation at Gilfach Colliery in 1907. The young lad sat on the wagon is Will Churchouse and his father, Mr. Jim Churchouse is standing on the far left with the shovel.

151. The ancient skills of the blacksmith are in progress here at Gilfach Colliery with Mr. Bill Thomas at the anvil. Mr. Thomas started his apprenticeship at Gilfach in 1929.

152. A further picture of Gilfach's 'smithies' and left to right are Dai Jones, Cecil Cox and Bill Thomas in about 1930.

153. The pit horse was an invaluable member of any colliery workforce despite the many mechanical availabilities. Above 'Jumbo' is seen with his master John Howells at Bargoed Colliery in the 1920s.

154./155. Time for a 'breather' on the coal truck with wagon repairers Fred Powell and Jim Box. The lower photograph shows a passenger train hauled by a Panier 0-6-0 locomotive, having just passed Bargoed Colliery. Even today Bargoed's railway facilities are better than some South Wales valleys but it is hard to imagine how good they were years ago. The town was a centre of importance for railway traffic, forming the junction of the Brecon and Merthyr and Rhymney lines. Records show that eighty years ago the average passenger bookings at Bargoed station totalled some 40000 with an equivalent number of people coming into the town each month by rail alone!

156./157. The lifting of coal from Gilfach Colliery finally came to an end in the early 1930s. It was however, some thirty years later before the eventual decision was taken to dismantle the remaining buildings. These two pictures are from 1963 and as local residents will know, the one-time site has now been replaced by the construction of houses at St. Andrew's Close.

158./161. Four pictures that illustrate the atmosphere at a coalmine to the full. The scene is at Bargoed during the early part of the twentieth century.

162. A very early picture, possibly dating from the mid 1880s, of Bargoed Station. Some old buildings include the Junction Inn, later to be demolished to make way for a more spacious Junction Hotel, itself since removed. The background shows Caersalem Chapel and an absence of housing, later to appear at Aberbargoed.

163. The station in later years, the mid 1960s when the days of steam-powered trains were reaching the end of a long history. To be noted in this view is the old ticket office which stood next to the bridge and The Junction Hotel to the left.

CHAPTER 5

Churches & Chapels

164. A glimpse inside Hanbury Road Baptist Chapel with the deacons. Seen left to right are - Standing: Mr. C. Borrett, unknown, Mr. L. Paul, Mr. J. Simpson and Mr. A. Davies. Seated: Mr. B. Long, Mr. Thomas, Mr. Baber, Rev. E. Stephens, Mr. B. Rees, Mr. P. Williams and Mr. I. Thomas.

165. Members of Hanbury Road Baptist pause for a moment during an annual Whitsun March in Hanbury Road in the 1920s. On the left was the old Bon Marché shop.

166. The ladies belonging to Hanbury Road Baptist Sisterhood in the 1950s.

167. Hanbury Road Baptists walking past the point where Bargoed Library now stands. The picture dates from the mid 1950s.

168. Some familiar faces with Rev. Emlyn Stephens in the pews at Hanbury Road are: Mrs Stephens, Gareth Stephens, Percy Williams, Billy Rees, Claude Borrett, Isabel Brookes, Gerald Brookes, Kathleen Brookes, Sally Salter, Irene Sheasby, John Sheasby, Desmond Davies, Olwyn Hughes, David Bright, Jock Simpson, Emily Bright, Mr. Rees, Mr. Long, Alwyn Davies, Annette Borrett, Roy Tucker, Mrs. Tucker, Margaret and Howard Jones and Mrs. Clarice Thomas.

169. The Wesleyan Chapel in Wood Street Bargoed which is seen here in about 1910, prior to the building of the Central Methodist Hall to the right. The chapel is now a Chapel of Rest owned by D.J. Thomas and Sons Funeral Directors.

ORDER OF SERVICE for the
Laying of the Foundation Stone
of the Church of St. Margaret,
Gilfach,

BY

Mrs. R. J. M. TENISON

AND

Dedication

BY THE RIGHT REVEREND THE

LORD BISHOP OF LLANDAFF

———————

Tuesday, May 23rd, 1933, at 3 p.m.

170. A scene from the laying of the foundation stone at St. Margaret's Church Gilfach in May 1933. Amongst the dignitaries seen below are Fred Davies (Peoples' Warden), Rev. Canon J.O. Williams, F. Scandrett (Hairdresser), Mr. and Mrs. Mullet.

171. The date is Whitsun 1937 and the scholars of Ainon Baptist Chapel Gilfach are on their annual walk at the top of Park Place. Some faces to look for are Mr. I. Peters, Miss Fisher, T. Matthews, Miss K.E. Matthews, G. Nicholas, E. Flew, B. Roberts, Mr. Morris (Deacon), L. Meade.

172. The Salvation Army, which has enjoyed strong support in the town for well over a hundred years. The twenty-five strong band is pictured here in 1934.

173. This time it is the turn of the lady members of Bargoed's Salvation Army Concertina Band to be photographed. The era is probably around 1910.

174. The scene will be recognised as Church Place and the year is about 1957 with a Whitsuntide March in progress. The choirboys belong to St. Gwlady's Church and a few names are known such as Alan Lovell, Howard Quick, John Edwards, Warren Evans, Cyril Meadon and John Evans.

175. Almost forgotten in most of today's chapel congregations is the 'Band of Hope'. The boys and girls here belong to South Street Methodist Church, pictured in 1922.

176. The Sunday School at Hanbury Road Baptist Chapel in 1952 with quite a few well-known faces to be remembered. Back Row: Christine Richards, Gloria Norman, Megan Winstone, Linda Parry, Ken Hamer. Second Row: Lynne Griffiths, Roger Mapstone, David Waters, Rev. Emlyn Stephens, Mr. I. Thomas. Third Row: Susan Lewis, Geraint Stephens, Ron Fairfax, John Mapstone, Christine Davies, Elsie Williams. Front: Mrs. R. Adams, Marilyn Spring, Rosemary Cutliffe, June Box, Elwyn Lewis, Ian Kingsley, Noreen Jones, Margaret Simpson, Christine James, Wendy Evans.

177./178. Whilst both of these photographs are essentially of religious interest, they do also provide a glimpse of the street scenery at Bargoed as it was during the early years of the twentieth century. Above, the Baptists of Hanbury Road are passing Trafalgar Square in about 1915. Below, another crowd of worshippers are at the top of Hanbury Road. On the right of the photograph can be seen some gypsy caravans and this is the spot where the Library now stands.

179. A small gathering of former local vicars and curates. Left to right are Rev. Thomas Richards B.A. (the first vicar of Bargoed 1904-1920), Rev. William Phillips (curate at St. Paul's Brithdir 1905-1915), Rev. D.J. Davies (curate of St. Peter's Deri) and Rev. S.W. Williams (curate at St. Gwlady's Bargoed 1908-1912).

180. Ruth Street which is crowded with worshippers on the march sometime during the 1950s.

181. A look at the interior of Ainon Baptist Chapel Gilfach which was built in 1902, and at the pulpit is the chapel's first Minister, Reverend Mansel John. Before this church was completed services were held at a house owned by a Mrs. Cross in Margaret Street Gilfach. Early Baptisms at Ainon were conducted in the Baptizmal pool in the church garden.

182. Some elders pictured at Ainon in April 1924. Left to right they are - Back: J. Calvert, J. Rees, E.W. Lewis, T.J. John and E. Griffiths. Front: E. Calvert (Treasurer), Rev. C. Bowen (Pastor) and A. Edwards (Secretary).

183. A host of church members belonging to Central Hall Methodist church in about 1958.

CHAPTER 6

Schooldays

184. St. David's Day, March 1st is celebrated throughout the principality, particularly in its schools. Here are some members of the Dining Staff of Gilfach Girls' School pictured in 1969 with Mrs. Annie John, Miss Annie Maddox, Mrs. Dorothy Evans (standing) and cook Mrs. Nellie Jenkins (seated).

185. Gilfach Junior Boys' School 1940-1941. Not all the names are known but here are a few to recall - Back Row: Wally Roach, David Jones, Colin Walters, Theo Young and Paul Jones. Second Row: Brian Walters, Lyndon Phillimore, Doug Hurst, Royston Thomks, Philip Lloyd, Brenig Jones, Keith Harris, Howard Jones and Willy Churchouse. Front: Brynley Lewis, Freddie Fox, unknown and Tiny Kirby.

186. The Gymnastics Class at Gilfach Fargoed Junior School 1979. On the left is headmaster Mr. Meade with fellow teacher Mrs. Wright on the right. The girls are - Back Row: Karen Price, Michelle Heydon, Carolyn Pugh, Liza Wright and Sian Edwards. Front Row: Helen Poole, Jacqueline James, Susan Davies, Elizabeth Shorey, Joanne Coles, Claire Watts and Melanie Lynch.

187. A picture from Gilfach Fargoed Girls' School in the year 1918. On the left is teacher Miss Annie Jones with colleague Miss Roebottom on the right. Perhaps there are a few readers who will recognise a mother or grandmother amongst the girls whose names include - Doris Collins, Hilda Dyer, Irene Lewis. Doris Maddox, Kathleen Leyshon, Emily Coles, Morwyn Davies, Kitty Chinnock, Mary Thomas, Edna Riley, May Prosser, Ada Morgan, Elizabeth Turvey, Gwyneth Lewis, Leila Smith and Winnie Parry.

188. A choir at Bargoed North Secondary Modern School in 1950. Seated centre are Miss Cowes (Head) and fellow teacher Mrs. Mair Williams. Some of the girls are - Rita Harris, Roslyn Harris, Valmai Wheeler, Enid Jones, Pamela Walker, Rita Goode, Jean Hodgkins, Rita Pritchard, Melita Davies, Janet Frowen, Valerie Lloyd, Iris Williams, Glenys Coles, Cynthia Potter, Jean Howard, Jean Crane, Maureen Powell, Brenda Clapham, Mary Davies, Daphne Toone, Pamela Harris, Sheila Benfield, Shirley Smallman, Marina Phillips, Betty Davies, Joyce Lewis, Margaret Cross, Eileen Points, Jean Bidgway, Thelma Davies, Shirley Morgan, Doreen Pritchard, Mary Lucas, Gwyneth Evans, Margaret Woods and Shirley Price.

189. Bargoed South Junior Girls in 1948 and left to right are - Back: Maureen Dwyer, Elsa Davies, Barbara Padfield, Maureen Reynolds, Dawn Morgan, Ann Gillard, Jean Jones, Pamela Fussell, Megan Jones and Doreen Winstone. Middle: Elaine Morgan, Dafrine Lewis, Maureen Ellcot, Wendy Smith, Marion Davies, Shirley Williams, Gillian Evans, Joan Baker, Wendy Shill and Claudia Barnette. Front: Valerie Evans, Elunid Morgan, Edna Weaver, Barbara Hurst, Sonia Sheen, ?, Margaret Derrick, Jean Smart and Irene Stockdale.

190. The years move on to 1958 at the Junior Girls and the pupils now are - Back: Christine James, Dawn Davies, Judith Pipe, Sandra Roberts, Sandra Short, Susan Lewis, Mary Jones, Mary Miles, Linda Boobyer, Geraldine Knight, Eirwen Ashford and Pat Marshall. Middle: Jillian Pine, Janie Johnson, Jeanette Treble, Christine Evans, Megan Eynon, June Box, Eileen Jones, Lynne Price, Pat Kelk, Diane Vaughan, Angela Assarati and Jackie Andrews. Front: Margaret Harris, Vivienne Jones, Mair Lewis, Anne McCarthy, Elizabeth Infram, Christine Woods, Jillian Rowlands, Dorothy Morgan, Carol Davies and Jean Weaver.

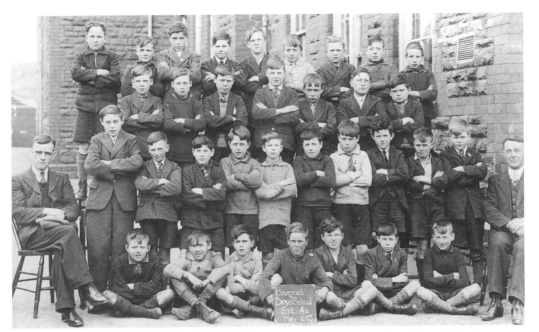

191. Standard IV at Bargoed North Boys' Elementary School in May 1953. Sat on the left is teacher Mr. T. Jones with headmaster Mr. E. Davies on the far right. The pupils are - Back: B. Jubilee, O. Norman, J. Brown, D.R. Jones, W. Hancocks, C. Rogers, H. Pugh, T. Rees, Unknown. Second Row: G. Grayson, A.H. Gibson, ?, R. Colly, G. Price, W. Prestide. Third Row: R. Tuck, A. Kent, W. Wallace, R. Jones, F. Shirley, R. Rees, ?, ?, L Thompson, S. Jones. Front: T. Atkinson, I. Hancocks, K. Yeo, ?, ?, E. Willots, A. Stevens.

192. Bargoed South Girls' School Scholarship Class 1937 and the girls are - Back: Muriel Board, Miss Taswell, Mair Batty, Betty Kedward, Betty Symes, Ada Goode, Marjorie Oates. Second Row: Lil Chilton, Doreen Reed, Beryl Jones, Kitty Maher, Eira Sallis, Doreen Hall, Enid Morgan, Dilys Clarke. Front: Mary Jones, Marjorie Coombes, Beryl Davies, Eira Lewis, Audrey Jones.

193. Teacher Mrs. Isaac with the pupils of Gilfach Infants' School in 1930. Back: A. Smith, I. Harris, I. Jones, T. Allway, D. Watkins, M. Jones, J. Bevan, F. Rice, R. Silverthorne. Second Row: C. James, H. Thomas, ?, ?, ?, J.G. Jones, J.M. Jones, G. Sloggart, M.Howells. Third Row: W. Evans, M. Allsop, P. McQuade, ?, B. Williams, ?, M. Pugh, B. Horton, C. Trigg. Front: S. Williams, S. Morgan, A. Morgan, D. Harding, M. Thomas, P. Walker, ?, H. Baker.

194. Teacher Mrs. Bowen with Class III at Gilfach Infants' in 1933. Back: Morwyn Matthews, Silvie Verity, Gwyneth James, ?, ?, Nancy Coates, Joan Davies. Second Row: Brynley Davies, Ivor Kinnersley, Gerald Wadman, ?, Margaret Thorley, Reg Hall. Third Row: Isobel Lambert, Terry Jones, ?, Ron Morgan, Betty Pratten, Evelyn Lewis, May Pine. Front: Cyril Watkins, Rebecca Levi, Mavis Williams, ?, Haulwen Humphries, Margaret Jones, Gwenllian John.

195. Gilfach Fargoed Junior School in 1970. The teacher at the time was Miss Fudge and the youngsters are - Back: Susan Lewis, Caroline James, Claire Sallis, Susan Whitcombe, Maxine Hennesy, Deborah Gough, Melinda Griffiths, Denise Blow, Helen Jones. Middle: Stephen Walwyn, Ian Watt, David Viles, Brian Jones, Robert Flanigan, Philip Diamond, Alan Faulkener, Mark Hayward, Keith Baines, Ivor Osborne, Gary Evans. Front: Wendy Waters, ?, Jane Woolridge, ?, Diane Oliver, Andrea Davies, Susan Jones, Kay Mills, Julie Thomas.

196. Gilfach Boys' School with teacher Mr. Amwel Jones in the1950s and the boys are - Back: ?, Jeffrey Cox, John Goldsworthy, Mike Walsh, Ivan Hollifield, Malcolm Bidgway, Glyn Terry, John Thomas, ?. Middle: Brian Jones, David Horton, David Honeybun, Alan Bye, ?, Ross Loveday, Terry Cushion, Jeff Davies. Front: David While, Bernard Horne, Robert Evans, Billy Summers, Robert Watkins, Alan Thomas, Grenville James, Colin Williams.

197. St. Gwlady's Infants' School 1965 and here are a few names which the author has identified. Girls - Sian Lewis, Julie Mudge, Amanda Williams, Kim Parry, Anita Jones, Susan Slatter, Barbara Evans, Janet Chidgey, Julie Fealy. Boys - Robert Doulton, Colin Thomas, Paul Gilbert, Christopher Morris, Kerry Hogan, Julian Adams, Wayne Price, Keith Jones, Colin Jones, Brent Thomas, Charles Griffiths, Stephen Conway.

198. St. Gwlady's Infants' School 1970 and amongst the group are Back: Heather Dix, Lindsay Edwards, Geraldine Thomas, Michelle Ball, John Lewington, Wendy France, Jane Tasker, Tracy Jarman, Michelle Daley. Middle: Michael Harries, Neil Cook, David Williams, Ian McCarthy, Mark Parry, David Richards, John Winston, Catherine Denner. Front: Michelle Cook, Denise Keating, Sian Evans, Yasmin Plange, Paula Hitchman, Gillian Gibson, Theresa Coles.

Sporting Memories

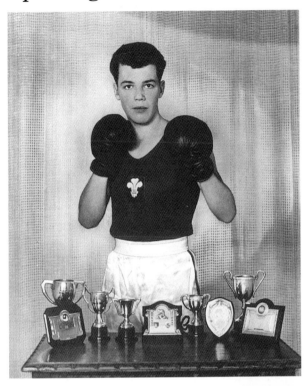

199. What will be a familiar figure to the boxing fraternity and local enthusiasts is that of Bargoed boy Ray Gabriel. He is pictured here with a few of his cups and trophies. Among his numerous achievements were flyweight champion of Wales in 1956, bantam-weight finalist in 1957 and British Railways Western Region Championship of Great Britain finalist, also in 1957.

200. Another talented boxer emanating from Bargoed was Alan Ball who is pictured on the right during the 1960s. Amongst his accomplishments were Welsh Schoolboy Champion, Welsh Junior and Senior Champion. In 1967 he became the A.B.A. middle-weight senior champion after defeating Chris Finnegan.

201. Some junior cricketers from Graig School in 1978-79 with accompanying teachers Mr. Tim Jones (left) and Mr. Hugh Nicholls (right). The boys are - Back: Paul James, Kevin Powell, Nicholas Powell, Trevor Chard and Kevin Harley. Front: Adrian Preece, Philip Phelps, Kevin Mills, Robbie Bowen and David Williams. Seated: Conrad Hayden and Jason Cooper.

202. From the 1950s are seen a few members of Bargoed Golf Club. Standing are - Dr. Arthur Richards, ?, J. Stanley Jones and Lance Jones. Seated: ?, Stan Hughes, Mr. Dash and Percy Williams.

203. The finalists of a season at Gilfach Tennis Club during the 1950s. Back Row: Greta Walters, Muriel Walters, Bill Walters, Jean Rogers, John Rogers, Mavis Barry, Gerald Barry and Joan Thompson. Front Row: Les Thompson (Secretary), Eric Whiting, Alan Matthews, Ron Jones, Rita Jones, Gaynor Morris, Brian Gough and Wynford Phillips (Treasurer).

204. Mr. Harry Andrews stands amidst a 1982 ladies' bowling team from Gilfach. The ladies standing are Lily Jones, Susan Knight, Doreen Andrews, Pat Czarnecki, Rita Jones, Sheila Heath and Margaret Price. Seated are Georgina Saunders, Lorna Perry, Audrey Mullens, Mary Powell, Olga Williams and Pat Walters.

205. Bargoed North Boys' School Rugby Team, under 14s 1959-60. Standing: Lyn Jones, Victor Watkins (Charlie), Ken Davies, Paul Frankos, Dicky Phillips, David Roberts, Derek Nelson and Mr. Phil Mantle (Teacher). Seated: Les Davies, Alwyn Jenkins, Roy Temple, Graham Parsons, Peter Moyle (Captain and Welsh Youth Cap), Andrew Duggan, Phil Waythe and Desmond Ramsey.

206. The Gilfach Y.M.C.A. Football Team of 1954. In the back row are Gwyn Lewis, Glan Lewis, Brian Lewis, Jimmy Verity, Bryn Matthews, Aubrey Eaketts, Tony Kirby, Bryn Perry, Don Howells, Bill Honey. Front: Joe Burrows (Secretary), Bryn Lewis, Ernie Crick, David Jones, Brian Edwards, Gerald Evans, Don Thomas, Jack Hughes (Chairman).

207. A good season for Gilfach Y.M.C.A. as they display the winning trophy in 1948-49. Standing are Reny Davies, Don Howells, David Lewis, John Burgess, Aubrey Eaketts, Keith Goodenough, Cyril Huxley, C.B. Best (Leader), Cled Jones (Coach). Seated: Dai Jones, Trevor Morgan, Jimmy Thomas, Ray Davies, Roy Jones, Joe Heath.

208. Gilfach Bargoed Y.M.C.A. Under 16s, Welsh Cup winners in the 1953-54 season. In the back are G. David, Mr. Hughes (President), Joe Burrows (Secretary), Alan Howells, Dai Thomas, Tudor Davies (Goal), G. Williams, Conrad Mills, Len Jones, Kerry Pitt. Front: C. Pope, G. Harris, Colin Hancox, Ken Williams, G. Davies and Graham Moore who later played for Wales.

209. Bargoed United Football Team seen here after winning the South Wales and Monmouthshire Amateur Cup 1945-46. Continually reading left to right the gentlemen are A. Kedward, D. Harding, L. Smith, M. Jones, R. Faulkener, E.D. Williams, F. Rawlings, J. Carter, C.C. Edwards, W. Edwards, T. Evans, W. Walters, W.R. Death, R.G. Weston, J. James, A.E. Oliver, J. Evans, B. Bridges, E. Davies, I.D. Hicks, G. Harding, R. Williams, I Jones, J. Puckey, J. Farmer and G. Winters.

210. A rather early photograph of Gilfach Football Club from the season 1904-05 and the kit, amongst many other things to do with the game, has come a long way since.

211. A popular event in years gone by was the Annual Gala held by Bargoed Swimming Club. The above scene is from the 1950s when there was no such luxury as indoor pools and leisure centres. The area is now a green-field play area.

212. A special occasion to mark a presentation to Mrs. Gwen Smart upon her retirement as swimming coach and lifeguard at Bargoed baths from 1937 to 1980. With Mrs. Smart are John Muscott (Under Manager), Robert Gordon (Attendant), John Price (General Manager), Stephen Andrews (Attendant) and Mr. Brenig Jones (Supervisor).

213. Bargoed Bathing Club members with their Rhymney Valley trophies in 1949-50. Left to right are Emrys Williams, Colin Barnett, Marcia Williams, Gwen Smart, Alan Evans, Windsor Roberts, Denny Miller and John Pepper.

214. Bargoed RFC in the season 1948-49. The back row consists of D. Hurd, J. Carter, J. Ashcroft, G.H. Davies, J. Fell and M. Jones. Middle: R. Gwylym, E. Mullins, G. Newman, J. Tippet, D. Baker, M. Tingle and L. Davies. Front: A. Baxondale and D. Watkins.

215. The Bargoed XV displaying their Mid-District Cup in 1964-65 and reading left to right from the back are seen J. Taysome, C. Jenkins, K. Rogers, R. Nelson, G. Webb, I. Richard, P. Ridley, B. Vowles, D. Bishop, P. Freeman, T. Lewis, G. Williams, H. Carter, G. Palmer, G. Adams, G. Grist, J. Holder, B. Price, M. Lewis and G. Evans.

216. The Bargoed Select Flying Pigeon Club in the 1960s. Back Row: Edwin Powell, Reg Acreman, Charlie Evans (Cockles), Arthur Morgan, Ivor Williams, Bill Powell, Joe Whetter, Bill Gatefield. Middle: Ted Burgess, Fred Acreman, Sid Duggan, Harry Clayton, Dai Lacey, Tom Horton, Sid Helps, John Lacey, Percy Brownswood, Reg Horton. Front: ?, Horace Lovett, Mike Hart (President), Tommy Smart (Chairman), Bill Bates (Secretary), Fred Powell, Charlie Thomas.

217. It's Trophy time for the Pigeon Club members at the prizegiving dinner party held at the Ex Servicemen's club in 1973. Back Row: R. Howells, F. Powell, T. Mills, E. Powell, F. Norman, K. Davies, B. McDuff, E. Williams, D. Williams, C. Robert, J. Early, G. Maher, A. Reed. Front Row: C. Cooper, J. Cooper, D. Mudge, S. Davies, J. Mac, B. Hall, T. Earley, H. Roberts.

218. Gwerthonor Workmen's Club Skittle Team posing for the cameraman after winning the South Wales Championships during the 1970-71 season. Seen left to right are - Back: A. Richards, Eric Rogers, Mog Price, T. Mounty, E. Price, Peter Price and Ianto Lewis. Front: Peter Powell, Ivor Powell, J. Pickering (Captain), Peter Gilbert and Ray Powell.

219. The Bargoed Social Club (Church Place) Rifle Team seen with some glittering prizes in the 1930s. Some of the markmen's names have been traced as follows - Jim Jones, Bill Pascoe, Jack Driscoll, Jim Driscoll, Jim Farmer, Mr. Goldsworthy and Jack Williams (Steward).

220. Another former sporting organisation was the Motorcycle Club. Here the Triangle Club of Gilfach line up for this photograph taken whilst camping at Monmouth in 1946. Riders and passengers are as follows S. Faulkener, G. Cross, S. Stuckey, E. Cross, W. Sault, D. Rees, H. Pugh, R. Shaw, W. Bartlett, K. Smith, C. Williams, S.V. Holloway, C. Huxley, G.L. Bowen.

221. Smiling faces at a South East Wales motorbike rally held at St. Fagan's in 1949 when Gilfach Triangle Club won their first team prize. The faces belong to W.H. Lerwill, Simon Stuckey, W.J. Pasmore, Joe Stuckey, B. Jones, G.L. Bowen, R.L. Southworth and A. Williams.

222. Gilfach Bargoed Y.M.C.A. Football Team in the season 1959-60. Back Row: Dai Gardiner, Brian Taswell, Peter Gilbert, Frank Watkins, Mal Smalley, Colin Coombes, Barry Horseman, Claude Borrett. Middle: John Hughes, Brian Edwards, Haydn Briggs, Phil McCarthy, Ron Hill, Gethin Jones. Front: Ron Turner and Granville Davies. Dai Gardiner it may be remembered went on to become a distinguished boxing promoter and a familiar face on the Televison screen.

223. The Y.M.C.A. Under 16s Football Team in the season 1967-68, photographed on the Basin Football Field, and the players are - Back: B. Horseman, A. Bradfield, N. Meredith, G. Jones, W. Price, M. Luther, G. Chappel, L. Jones, P. Maslin, G. Davies (Slip). Front: T. Prasowski, P. Franklin, J. Done, A. Shaw, G. Evans, J. Furtek.

224. The committee for the Welsh National Swimming Championships which were held at Bargoed Park in 1952. Amongst those to be seen are Mrs. Seabourne, Mr. Kedward, Dai Brown, Mrs Bernice Hooper, Mr. Hooper, Mrs. Morris (The Park), Mr. and Mrs. Smart, Mr. and Mrs. Cutcheon, Mr. and Mrs. Mason (Dentist), Mr. and Mrs. Ford, A.S. Williams J.P., Mr. E. Williams, Mr. Kerrigan (Baths Superintendent), Jack Martin and Mrs. Coslett (Chief Inspector).

225. Heolddu Comprehensive School 1st XV photographed outside the former Grammar School in the 1973-74 season with P.E. teacher Mr. Harris. Not all of the boys' names can be recalled but they do include B. Hopkins, Howard Smith, Nigel Davies, Roger Jones, Philip George, Ian Scanlon, K. Breeze, Philip Hurd, Andrew Hurd, G. Rees and Philip Pratten.

226. Gilfach Y.M.C.A. Under 14s Football Team seen on the field in 1978-79 and the names are - Back: John Bray (Trainer), Jeff Harris, Anthony Lewis, Wayne Pollard, Andrew Rees, Gavin Cushion, Anthony Lewis (Opal), Jonathan Duggan. Front: Martin Saunders, Paul Bye, Terry James, Graham Jones, Andrew Ashcroft and Lee Jones.

Acknowledgements

The author is grateful to the undermentioned for their valuable help in providing photographs and information used in this book. Sadly, one or two have passed away prior to publication and acknowledgement of their contribution is conveyed to their relatives. Apologies are offered to anyone who may have been inadvertently omitted.

Alan Ball, Bargoed Library, Mrs. G. Bartlett, Mrs. Borret, Mr. and Mrs. Les Bowen, Mrs. C. Box, Miss L. Chilton, Mr. W.J. Churchouse, Mr. Alan Dando, Alwyn Davies, John Dines, Mr. M. Dutton, Glenys Edwards, John Edwards, Ivor Evans, Brian Faulkener, Ray Gabriel, Sarah Grist, Mr. and Mrs. Ron Heath, Mrs. Hill, Pamela Hopkins, Mrs. G. Horton, Mr. and Mrs. John Howells, Mr. and Mrs. John James, Mr. L. Jenkins, David Jones, Lyn Jones, Noel Jones, Mrs. Keacher, Mrs. D. King, Pam Lambe, Mrs. E. Lawrence (New Zealand), Mrs. Margaret Lewis, Mrs. Marian Lewis (Bargoed Hall), Jean Lynch, Phil Maher, John Mayne, Valerie Mansell, Mr. and Mrs. J. Mathews, Mrs. A. Mayo, Mr. Ron Mills, Sandra Morgan, Doris Moss, Marian Mysiura, Jean Plange, Amanda Powell (BBC), Mrs. M. Powell, Leighton Powell, Graham Pratten, Wendy Rees, Mr. H. Riden, Beryl Rowlands, Mr. and Mrs. Tommy Sallis, Mrs. G. South, Mr. and Mrs. Joe Stuckey, Malcolm Thomas, Joan Thompson, Bill Thomas, Harold Trivett, Mrs. May Watkins, Mr. and Mrs. David While, Dr. David Williams, Olive Williams, Mrs. Eveline Withers (Queenie).